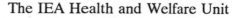

The IEA Health and Welfare Unit

Choice in Welfare Series No. 8

Saving Lives:
The NHS Accident and Emergency Service and How To Improve It

Saving Lives:
The NHS Accident and Emergency Service and How To Improve It

Peter J.F. Baskett
Miles Irving
Brian McKibbin
Sir Reginald Murley

London
The IEA Health and Welfare Unit
1991

First published in 1991
by
The IEA Health and Welfare Unit
2 Lord North St
London SW1P 3LB

ISBN 0-255 36269-2

Typeset by the IEA Health and Welfare Unit
Printed in Great Britain by
Goron Pro-Print Co. Ltd
Churchill Industrial Estate, Lancing, West Sussex

Contents

Editor's Foreword

The Editor's task in this Foreword is less demanding than usual since the three essays in this volume have benefited from a masterly introduction by Sir Reginald Murley, a distinguished founding member of our Advisory Council. But this would not be an IEA paper if I did not intrude at least a word or two of economic analysis to accompany the expert testimony of Sir Reginald and the three distinguished NHS consultants who have contributed to this publication.

Among the arguments advanced in favour of the NHS is the claim that an insurance-based system will not offer reliable emergency cover because hospitals will be reluctant to treat patients who are unable to pay. In this view, the hospital's first concern will be to perform a 'wallet biopsy' to establish ability to pay. Then, once the insurance status of the accident victim has been established, top-class care will follow for the insured and second-class care for the uninsured. It is therefore better, so the argument runs, to provide a state-funded accident and emergency service for all.

It goes without saying that the victims of accidents should receive the best that medical science can offer, but the NHS falls far short of this ideal: it offers a scandalously inadequate service which is a national disgrace. And, as the distinguished contributors to this volume all agree, we need to look overseas to the trauma centres of North America and Europe for examples of the best in accident and emergency care.

The NHS accident and emergency service is inadequate because of the long record of under-investment in the service by governments of all political persuasions since World War Two. The authors of the essays are professionally committed to the NHS and write from unrivalled medical experience which I commend to my fellow economists and others. For their part, I hope the authors will indulge an IEA editor for offering an economic comment on the failure of the NHS. Health care, in economic jargon, is said to be a luxury good because the wealthier people become the more they spend on medical services. Perhaps a better way to put this claim is to say that some health care is a necessity—with accident care the prime example—whilst some other medical interventions, such as tattoo removal, cosmetic surgery or fertility treatment, are discretionary. It is because there are a large and increasing variety of optional medical services from which patients might benefit that no government can ever hope to meet everyone's expectations from taxation. The practical outcome of promising to do so has been widespread dissatisfaction and constant rationing. And one tragic outcome of rationing within the NHS has been that the truly necessitous medical services for victims of accidents and emergencies have been provided inadequately or not at all.

Rising, uncosted expectations mean that severe doubt must remain whether this flaw in the NHS can ever be overcome whilst the NHS is funded overwhelmingly from taxation. The inescapable lesson is that, unless we permit a greater role for private finance, including insurance, Britain will always have an inferior accident and emergency service.

Despite political resistance this fundamental debate will not indefinitely be stilled. Meanwhile, within the authors' terms of reference, a strong case is made for increasing spending on the NHS accident and emergency service without radical reform of NHS funding. Leaving aside the controversy about how best to finance the NHS, the authors' criticisms of present arrangements and their recommendations for change are offered as timely and informed contributions to a neglected public debate about how to improve the NHS accident service.

David G. Green

Preface

The Health and Welfare Unit of the Institute of Economic Affairs is especially pleased to publish three important papers directed to the more efficient and cost-effective care of accident victims in the United Kingdom. Each is written by a distinguished specialist. Miles Irving, a general surgeon in Manchester, and chairman of an important working party at the Royal College of Surgeons of England puts forward a pungent argument for a change in priorities. The mortality cost of injury deaths, which tend to affect those in a lower and more productive age group, is almost four times that for cancer and six and a half times that for cardio-vascular disease; and yet, both in the U.S.A. and the U.K., inordinately smaller sums of money are invested in trauma care and research than are applied to cancer and cardiac disease. It may surprise the general reader to learn that, notwithstanding the remarkable recent improvement in survival figures for childhood leukaemia and certain less common cancers, there has been little or no improvement in overall survival for the commoner organ cancers. Irving, therefore, favours some redirection of resources from cancer and cardiovascular disease to trauma and advocates the development of some 25 major trauma centres in the UK. If this should seem too expensive he concedes that even eight such centres could result in significantly higher QUALY[1] scores than are presently gained for two now well accepted treatments; namely, those for kidney transplant and coronary artery by-pass grafting. He ends his paper with a brief consideration of the funding methods which might be used to achieve these aims.

Brian McKibbin, an orthopaedic surgeon who is head of the Accident and Orthopaedic Services in Cardiff, outlines the existing distribution of district and regional services in the UK, and the changed role of the orthopaedic surgeon due to the greatly increased operative fixation of fractures. Whilst conceding the case

---

[1] QUALY: Quality Adjusted Life Years, being a unit of measurement suggested by Professor Maynard, University of York.

for a few large regional trauma centres, where senior orthopaedic, general, cardiac, neurosurgical, plastic and maxillofacial specialists, would all be concentrated under one roof, he points out that the frequently irregular incidence of serious multiple injuries could hardly justify many such centres devoted *exclusively* to the care of accident victims. For this reason, and because of the singular lack of official response following many important published studies in the last forty years, he sees the way forward as best served by concentrating on district hospital services and regional centres.

Peter Baskett, a Bristol anaesthetist, prepared his important review of the UK system more than a year ago. Despite the Osmond-Clarke and Platt reports of the early 1960s' there was a total failure by the then Ministry of Health to implement any significant reforms. He goes on to quote some important retro-spective and prospective studies by expert professional assessors which exposed a significant and, indeed, unacceptably high incidence of preventable deaths. Such deaths were not only related to the frequently inadequate standards of pre-hospital care, but also to the sometimes poor hospital service. There is urgent need for wider training of ambulance paramedics; for possible extension of the GP emergency service pioneered by Dr Kenneth Easton, of Catterick, and for the wider use of mobile hospital teams and helicopter evacuation. Dr Baskett's strictures on what I have elsewhere called 'the barnacles of the new bureaucracy' are certainly fully justified.[1]

Much of this is, indeed, as Dr Baskett declares, 'a tale of woe' which some may be tempted to interpret as typical shroud-waving by the medical establishment. But, coming as I do from an earlier generation than our three authors, I have every reason to echo their criticisms and firmly support most of their recommendations. As a pre-war medical student in 1937 I decided to visit the Unfallkrankenhaus, in Vienna, the famous accident hospital directed by Lorenz Bohler and set up by the Accident Insurance

---

[1] Murley, Sir Reginald, Surgical Roots and Branches, *British Medical Journal*, London: The Memoir Club, 1990.

Office there. That institution had totally transformed the standards of fracture care for the tramway and railway workers, whilst ensuring more cost-effective care and earlier return to productive tax-paying work. There was nothing in the UK to compare with it. Qualifying, as I did, just before the second world war, and serving in the RAMC for six and a half years, it was not long before I was able to see the benefits and cost-effectiveness of our wartime army multi-specialist casualty service. From 1942, in Egypt, and later in North Africa and Italy, I was privileged to work in a plastic and maxillofacial surgical unit which was closely associated with neurosurgical and ophthalmic units both in the forward and base areas. The standards of individual and combined specialist care available to the wounded soldier were generally vastly superior to anything I was to find post-war in the UK, where there was progressive closure of many of the wartime Emergency Medical Service regional multi-specialist centres.

But there were some compensations. At the inception of the NHS in 1948, there were many young surgeons and anaesthetists freshly returned from the services who had had considerable experience of accident and war surgery. District hospitals up and down the country, as well as regional and teaching centres, were staffed by these men who were exceptionally well qualified to deal with civilian accident work. It was not until the late 1970s, as many of these doctors began to retire, that the inherent deficiencies of the NHS became more and more apparent. Failure to act upon the earlier recommendations of Osmond-Clarke and Platt then became even more blatantly evident. I firmly share many of the strongly expressed views and criticisms of our three authors and believe that the solution to our problems may require rather different handling in different parts of the UK. I strongly suspect that our centralised, inflexibly bureaucratic and monolithic system may be incapable of coming up with the right answers. Since it was the enlightened self-interest of one insurance company, and the workers it covered, which produced the Unfallkrankenhaus in Vienna, is it not possible that with the present opportunity for formation of independent hospital trusts in this country, some of our own insurance companies might find it profitable to invest in similar ventures over here? And could not a more enlightened use of our Road Fund ensure that governments directed substantially increased resources to this most worthy cause? Or have our health services for too long been in the hands of a government bureaucracy which is now as unwilling to devise more efficient and cost-effective solutions, as it is reluctant to measure the overall costs and benefits?

The constitution of the Institute of Economic Affairs requires its Trustees and Directors to disclaim any commitment to the analyses and conclusions of its authors. However, such inhibitions do not apply to those of us who are members of the Advisory Council of its Health and Welfare Unit. I strongly commend the papers of Miles Irving, Brian McKibbin and Peter Baskett as making important contributions to a vital debate, requiring urgent consideration by ministers, the medical profession and the general public.

Reginald Murley
President of the Royal College
of Surgeons of England, 1977-1980

The Authors

Peter J.F. Baskett is a Consultant Anaesthetist at Frenchay Hospital and the Royal Infirmary, Bristol and is Consultant Adviser to the Accident and Emergency Departments of these hospitals. He is also Senior Clinical Lecturer in Anaesthesia, University of Bristol; Lieutenant Colonel, Royal Army Medical Corps (TA); Honorary Civilian Adviser in Resuscitation to the British Army and Consultant Adviser to the Avon Ambulance Service.

He is at present President of the Association of Anaesthetists of Great Britain and Ireland, as well as President of the World Association for Emergency and Disaster Medicine and President of the European Resuscitation Council.

He is the author of approximately 70 articles and chapters on general anaesthetic matters, acute pain relief, resuscitation, immediate and critical care, paramedic training and disaster medicine. He is also the author and editor of four books on *Immediate Care, Resuscitation,* and *Disaster Medicine.*

Professor Miles Irving qualified from Liverpool University Medical School in 1959. He trained in surgery in Liverpool, Newcastle upon Tyne, Sydney, Australia and Birmingham prior to becoming Reader in Surgery and Honorary Consultant Surgeon to St Bartholomew's Hospital, London. He moved to Manchester in 1976 to take up the post of Professor of Surgery and Honorary Consultant Surgeon at Hope Hospital, Salford. He is currently Chairman of the School of Surgical Sciences at Manchester University; a member of the Council of the Royal College of Surgeons of England; Honorary Consultant Surgeon to the Army; a member of the General Medical Council and a member of several Department of Health Committees. He was Chairman of the Royal College of Surgeons Working Party which produced the report on the Management of Major Injuries. He is an Honorary Fellow of the American Association for the Surgery of Trauma and an Honorary Member of the British Association for Accident and Emergency Medicine.

Professor Brian McKibbin is currently Professor and Head of the Department of Traumatic and Orthopaedic Surgery, University of Wales College of Medicine in Cardiff and Honorary Consultant Surgeon to the South Glamorgan Area Health Authority having been appointed in 1971. He was formerly the Head of the University Department of Orthopaedics in Sheffield from 1967 to 1971.

He is at present an elected member of the Council of the Royal College of Surgeons of England and was formerly President of British Orthopaedic Research Society and of the British Orthopaedic Association. He is currently Chairman of the Trauma Committee of the latter which is at present preparing a survey of the management of orthopaedic trauma in Great Britain.

His clinical interests include orthopaedic trauma, spinal injuries and various aspects of children's orthopaedics. Research interests include the biology of fracture healing and the development of new materials as implants for fracture treatment.

Introduction: A Case for a Change in Priorities

Miles Irving

Slowly but surely, the public, the medical profession, the media and politicians are beginning to appreciate that provision of health care is subject to financial constraints, with all the implications this has for access to treatment. Increasingly it is appreciated that not everything that is technically possible in the sphere of medical treatment can be made universally available in even the wealthiest of societies.

Limitation of access to treatment has long been recognised as a necessity by the military surgeon on the battlefield who, through a clinical classification system known as triage, restricts the most effective treatments to those who will obtain the greatest benefit. Yet this logical approach, readily accepted as commonsense in times of war, is all but abandoned in peacetime in favour of decisions based upon emotion, fashion, and political pressure.

The situation we face in the Western world, of rising demands from an increasingly ageing population reliant on resources generated by a diminishing workforce, has many analogies with the battlefield scenario. Rice and Mackenzie in their report to the United States Congress on 'The cost of injury'[1] asked 'where, in

---

[1] Rice, D.P. and MacKenzie, E.J., *Cost of Injury in the United States: A Report to Congress*. San Francisco, CA: Institute for Health and Ageing, University of California and Injury Prevention Center, John Hopkins University.

such a situation, health care priorities should be placed?'. Their answer is to place priorities where there is likely to be the greatest improvement in welfare or well-being. How does the National Health Service measure up to such a philosophy? It is my belief that our present priorities in the acute sector are seriously flawed and that the provision of clinical services and the allocation of research funds show an illogicality that is difficult to justify when one analyses the facts in the manner suggested in the report to Congress. Nowhere is this more evident than in the contrast between the relative allocation of resources to the treatment of, and research into, cancer and the treatment of, and research into, the injured.

Whereas injury is primarily a disease of the first four decades of life (indeed it has been described as the last great plague of the young) malignant disease is mainly a problem of those aged over sixty. Only 1.3 per cent of cancers occur in those under the age of twenty five. The small proportion that do develop in the under sixties, with the notable exception of breast cancer, are often of the leukaemia/lymphoma variety which are relatively successfully treated by existing techniques. Unfortunately there is little evidence that treatment of the vast majority of cancers makes any difference to outcome. Bailar and Smith in 1986[1] commenting on the overall changes in mortality from cancer in the USA since 1950 stated that there was no evidence that some 35 years of intense and growing efforts to improve the treatment of cancer have had much overall effect on the most fundamental measure of clinical outcome, i.e. death. Indeed with respect to cancer as a whole they felt that ground had been lost, as shown by the rise in age-adjusted mortality rates in the entire population. The fact that most cancers occur towards the end of an individual's natural life means that even if a 'cure' were found it would make little difference to the health of the population in terms of prolongation of life and virtually no difference to the economic welfare of the community in terms of reduction of lost working days. On both

---

[1] Bailar, J.C. and Smith, E.M., Progress Against Cancer?, *New England Journal of Medicine*, Vol. 314, 1986, pp. 1226-1232.

counts this is markedly different to injury which primarily affects a section of society where a life saved and restored to the previous state of health means restoration to useful economic activity. Figures from the United States demonstrate the disproportionate economic effect of injury upon the community compared with other common illnesses and equally disproportionate response in terms of allocation of research funds. Thus the mortality cost of an injury death in the USA is estimated at $335,000 which is almost four times that for cancer and six and a half times that for cardiovascular disease. In contrast research expenditure on injury by all federal agencies amounted to $160 million in 1987 which is about one tenth of that spent on cancer research and one sixth of that spent on cardiovascular research.

In the United Kingdom at the present time the situation is probably worse, with only one per cent of the Medical Research Council budget being spent on injury research. The priority given to research into cancer and its treatment might be justified if it could be demonstrated that useful results were being achieved. Sadly, with the one or two exceptions this is not the case. Indeed so dismal are the results in both areas that recently Temple and Burkitt[1] have suggested that most current cancer research be abandoned and that there should be redirection of effort into prevention which is the only area where there is hope of advance in the field of malignant disease.

Despite the facts outlined above we read of the planned establishment at The Hammersmith Hospital of yet another centralised cancer treatment and research unit in London to complement the existing centres. This is in marked contrast to the absence of any unit in London devoted to basic research into injury, its consequences or prevention.

As has been clearly pointed out in the accompanying papers, injury is the major cause of death and morbidity in the economically most active section of our community—the under 35s—and

---

[1] Temple, N.J. and Burkitt, D.P., The War On Cancer—Failure of Therapy and Research: Discussion Paper, *Journal of the Royal Society of Medicine*, Vol. 84, 1991, pp. 95-98.

4

this group is responsible for more deaths and lost working days than heart disease and cancer combined. Yet when it comes to publicising this fact the media lack interest, preferring always to highlight the problem of malignant disease.

The intellectual dishonesty of the media in this respect is nowhere better demonstrated than in the case of the possible association between leukaemia and radiation. Banner headlines and cartoons depicting skulls were the response, even in the broadsheet newspapers, to the revelation of a small cluster of leukaemia cases around Sellafield. Yet, what are the facts? In the 15 years between 1974 and 1988 the West Cumbrian Health district recorded the deaths from leukaemia of eight people under the age of 25. In the same period 158 people in the same age group in the same health district died from injury and associated untoward events. *The Times* chose not to publish this information even in their correspondence columns. Until the media decide that injury is a serious hazard to the health of our community it is unlikely that we will see the widespread development of trauma centres and other facilities for the care of the injured, the case for which has been so cogently argued in the accompanying papers.

One of the objections frequently advanced against the establishment of trauma centres is the cost. Recently O'Kelly and Westaby[1] have carried out a detailed study of the economic aspects of trauma care in general, and trauma centres in particular, using published and locally obtained financial data. Information derived from North American patient populations similar to those experienced in this country (i.e. 55-83 per cent blunt trauma, mostly from road traffic accidents) showed that survivors admitted to a trauma centre would spend about 28 days in hospital, 50 per cent being in an intensive care unit. On discharge from hospital 20 per cent of the survivors had regained their pre-injury functional state, the remainder requiring longer because of physical, social, education, and economic factors. However, one year after injury

[1] O'Kelly, T.J. and Westaby, S., Trauma Centres and the Efficient Use of Financial Resources, *British Journal of Surgery*, Vol. 77, 1990, pp. 1142-1144.

80 per cent of survivors are independently mobile and 57 per cent of those in work before injury have returned to previous employment. Two and a half years after injury 78 per cent of those severely injured (Injury Severity Score >15) are judged to have achieved a good outcome with no disability. Seventy per cent will have regained their former work status and more will return to work eventually. Up to ten per cent remain severely disabled and requiring assistance but only one to two per cent survive in a vegetative state.

O'Kelly and Westaby, having demonstrated what can be achieved by centralised treatment of injury then turn to the cost of providing trauma centres. They base their calculations on a network of only eight centres in contrast to the 25 recommended in the Royal College of Surgeons report. The eight centres would each admit about 1,000 cases a year. Using data derived from the Oxford Regional Neurosurgery unit, where intensive care costs £1,500 per day and a ward bed £250 a day, they demonstrate that the cost per life saved based upon a 28-day stay with continuous in-house consultant supervision from five specialties would be £31,268. They calculate the cost of building, commissioning and maintaining each trauma centre would be £1 million per year for ten years. O'Kelly and Westaby then go on to analyse the benefits that can be obtained from sophisticated trauma care using the QUALY (Quality Adjusted Life Years) approach. They calculate that the 78 per cent of survivors who make a good functional recovery after trauma centre care would have a QUALY score of 0.9 whilst the ten per cent of survivors making only a moderate recovery would score at least 0.7. The cost per QUALY gained per centre would be £942. They contrast this with the value of extra service costs per QUALY gained for two well-accepted treatments, namely kidney transplantation (£3,000) and coronary artery bypass grafting (£1,270).

Whilst trauma centres would undoubtedly be expensive, costing between £68 and £100 million per year depending upon the number of centres established, and the cost per life saved between £31,000 and £46,000, the expenditure would be well worth it when one considers the economic consequences to the community of restoring an individual to productive work. In conclusion, the authors reiterate that survivors from trauma centre care are young, that most achieve a good quality of life, return to their previous work and enjoy a life expectancy equal to that of an uninjured subject of the same age.

On this evidence, trauma centres are an efficient use of resources and would be funded preferentially if strict economic criteria were applied. In the light of this evidence those responsible for the allocation of resources must explain on what basis they are willing to support the centralisation of services for cancer treatment and transplantation but not for the injured, other than one underfunded pilot study.

Whilst everyone acknowledges that the cost of establishing centralised trauma services will, to begin with, be considerable there are ways to finance such centres. Transfer of resources is the obvious one but if this is politically unacceptable then a levy on the road fund tax, employed by the Australian state of Victoria to finance the magnificent trauma centre at the Alfred Hospital, or a levy on insurance companies should provide the necessary funding.

If the economic and humanitarian arguments for a redirection of resources into the management and rehabilitation of the injured are clear, the arguments for a major investment in the prevention of injury are overwhelming. Yet once again the media and politicians lack interest. When the Royal College of Surgeons report on the management of major injuries was produced there was at least significant media interest for a short time. However, a subsequent, and possibly even more important report on accident prevention[1] was to all intents and purposes ignored.

Publicity aimed at preventing the spread of AIDS has been extensively funded yet the much bigger problem of injury, which is currently killing one hundred people each week in the United Kingdom from road accidents alone, remains without significant prevention campaigns. It is a sobering thought that during the

---

[1] *Accident Prevention—A Social Responsibility*, Royal College of Surgeons of England, 1989.

seven months between the invasion of Kuwait and the end of the Gulf war around a quarter of a million citizens of the EC were killed or injured by accidents in their own countries. This is in marked contrast with what happened to the coalition forces on the supposedly more dangerous desert battlefields. Legislation already passed concerning the wearing of seat belts and motorcycle helmets has proved its value in preventing injury, yet other measures which could be equally effective such as helmets for cyclists, lower speed limits, cycle paths and a total driving ban on those causing accidents through alcohol abuse remain outside the law.

All this evidence shows that there is need for a change in priorities if we are to achieve adequate services for the care of the injured and make inroads into the prevention of injury.

2

Trauma Care:
A Tale of Woe

Peter J.F. Baskett

The Magnitude of the Problem

In the UK trauma is the commonest cause of death in both males and females between the ages of one and 35 years. Road traffic accidents head the list of causes. More than 5,100 died on the roads in 1987—almost 100 per week, every week[1]—a number greatly exceeding the carnage at Hillsborough Football Ground on that fateful Saturday in May 1989. Even more staggering is the number of seriously injured—over 64,000 in 1987. Each of these patients stayed 10-12 days in hospital, accounting for approximately 700,000 bed days that year. For every death on the roads there are more than two victims with permanent disability. In addition, almost as many die from injury in the home as on the roads, although these incidents occur in different age groups—infants and the elderly. Industrial accidents account for a further 26,000 hospital admissions annually.[2]

These numbers do not include the headline-hitting incidents, such as rail and air crashes, terrorist explosions and hand-gun injuries which, even in Northern Ireland, account for only a small

---

[1] Extracts from Hansard (February-July 1989). Compiled by The Parliamentary Advisory Council for Transport Safety, 1989.

[2] Westaby, S., *Trauma—Pathogenesis and Treatment*, Oxford: Heinemann, 1989.

proportion of the total numbers of dead and injured. Only 49 died in 1984 in the UK from gunshot wounds—many of them accidental. By contrast, in 1982 in the USA, there were 11,000 murders and a further 10,000 accidental deaths or suicides involving handguns.

By virtue of the fact that road accidents and industrial injury involve the young and middle aged, the ensuing socio-economic effects are particularly disturbing. In this productive age group there is not only the enormous cost of treatment, rehabilitation and welfare support of the dependants (in most cases borne by the State) but there is also a substantial loss of talent in the work place and reduction in tax revenue to compound the economic disaster.

The Department of Transport[1] has calculated the average cost of a fatality due to a road accident in 1987 to be more than £500,000. Thus the total figure for the 5,000 plus who die on our roads amounts to over £2.5 billion. Add to this the cost of fatal injuries in industry, in the home and from murder and manslaughter, plus the cost of non-fatal injuries, and the figure becomes quite staggering—over one per cent of the Gross National Product.

The price of trauma cannot only be measured in terms of cash but also in lost talent to the nation and in physical and psychological debility in survivors and their relatives and loved ones.

The recovery from psychosomatic illness or overlay attributed to trauma is often protracted by legal delays in coming to settlements in claims of negligence.

The Background to the UK System of Trauma Care

Since before the inception of the National Health Service in 1948, it has been appreciated that the management of trauma in the UK has been, to put it kindly, sub-optimal.

In 1943 the British Orthopaedic Association produced a memorandum identifying the need for properly organised hospital

---

[1] Department of Transport, *Highways Economic Note No. 1*, October 1988; (APMI p. 1081-1014), *Road Accident Costs 1987*.

facilities for the management of trauma and proposed that orthopaedic surgeons should have overall responsibility for these patients. Further articles followed in the literature recommending that comprehensive accident services be established by each Regional Hospital Board. Little progress was made in achieving these goals and in the early sixties both the BMA and the Ministry of Health set up Committees to review the nation's Accident Service. The BMA Committee was chaired by Sir Henry Osborne Clarke, who concluded that there was no regional organisation, there was under-funding of accommodation and staffing and there were too many small casualty departments. They suggested a three-tier service with general practitioners treating minor injuries in their surgeries, the district hospital casualty department staffed by orthopaedic surgeons treating the majority and the creation of regional specialist units for the complex major multiple injured (equivalent in concept to today's trauma centre).

The Ministry of Health's Medical Advisory Committee set up a working party chaired by Sir Harry Platt. This working party reported in 1962 and, by and large, agreed with the Osborne Clarke proposals although they suggested that the casualty department should be re-named the accident and emergency unit. While approving of the arrangement of orthopaedic surgeons having responsibility for the service in district hospitals they did not recommend the creation of accident surgery or specialist accident hospitals.

In fact only one specialist accident hospital has ever existed in the United Kingdom—The Birmingham Accident Hospital—and this achievement was due almost entirely to the vision, talent and tenacity of Sir William Gissane and Mr Peter London, supported by local business and citizens. The experience and contribution of The Birmingham Accident Hospital staff is quite unique and represented the gold standard of care in the sixties. However, as the potential for treatment of the seriously injured improved with the contribution of neuro, cardiothoracic, genito-urinary and maxillo-facial surgery and a comprehensive anaesthesia, resuscitation and intensive care service, it became clear that specialist accident hospitals could no longer exist in isolation but required to be attached to a major centre, housing all the appropriate allied specialties. Successive Regional Hospital Boards and Health Authorities failed to respond to this blueprint for a first class service and the Birmingham Accident Hospital currently struggles on, miserably under-funded and unsure of its future, supported only by a dedicated staff who work—incredibly in this day and age—without a CT scanner. Surely this has been an opportunity lost for over a decade and a half for Britain to create an outstanding trauma centre and gain priceless experience of its value during that time. In 1991 we start from scratch.

Meanwhile, the nation's Accident Service muddled along under the, perforce, rather tenuous supervision, of the orthopaedic surgeons who found that they were unable to devote adequate time to the service due to other commitments in their specialty. They also found themselves ill trained to care for the large proportion of patients who attend accident and emergency departments with cardiovascular, thoracic and psychiatric disease. Consequently, the departments were largely staffed by inexperienced trainees unsupervised by consultants and by doctors in the sub-consultant grade, many of whom had to learn 'on the job' as they went along.

As a result of this most unsatisfactory situation, the Joint Consultants' Committee set up a Working Party chaired by Sir John Bruce in 1971 to review, once again, the Accident and Emergency Services. This group recommended the creation of the specialty of accident and emergency medicine with a formal training programme. The new specialty was accepted by the powers-that-be after some squabbling over territory amongst the doctors who did not wish their beds or surgical territory to be encroached upon. Nevertheless, the new specialty was approved in its infancy by the Joint Consultative Committee's Working Party on Medical Staffing in the Accident and Emergency Services, chaired by Walpole Lewin, which reported in 1978. This Working Party also commented on the need for a wide breadth of training for the new specialty and indicated that trainees could be recruited from anaesthesia and medicine, as well as from surgery.

After remarkably slow progress over almost 20 years, due partly to lack of suitable trainees, but more particularly due to lack of funding in competition with other specialties, the majority of district general hospitals now have at least one such consultant in post. Few hospitals have more than one post and as a result many of the accident and emergency departments of our nation's hospitals still do not have a consultant presence for much of the 24 hours and the work is left to trainees and clinical assistants who work on a long lead away from supervision.

It took a number of factors to instigate the next formal enquiry into Britain's management of its trauma victims. Reports from other countries clearly indicated that they were devoting a considerably greater proportion of health care resources to help trauma victims than was the UK. Pre-hospital care in the United States was provided by highly trained paramedics, an arrangement which stemmed from the experience of their value in the Vietnam War. This example in principle had been followed in Australia and South Africa. In Europe emphasis was placed on a physician-based service which has achieved remarkably high standards in the Federal Republic of Germany, in France with the SAMU and SMUR systems, in Belgium and in many of the Eastern Bloc countries, notably Czechoslovakia and Hungary.

In Britain during the late 1970s and 1980s, a pre-hospital care service which could be said to be of an adequate standard only existed in a small number of specific locations. In certain areas paramedic training schemes had been started and produced good results[1] but many systems initially confined their work to the care of cardiac patients as the benefit of ECG monitoring and early electric shock treatment known as defibrillation had become well established.[2] In the early days, indeed up to the mid-1980s, such schemes did not have Department of Health encouragement because of fears of financial consequences and trade union

---

[1]   Baskett, P.J.F., Diamond, A.W., Cochrane, D.F., 'Urban Mobile Resuscitation—Training & Service', *British Journal of Anaesthetists*, 1976, 48: pp. 377-385.

[2]   Chamberlain, D.A., White, N.M., Binning, R.A., Parker, W.S. & Kimber, E.R., 'Mobile Coronary Care provided by Ambulance Personnel', *British Heart Journal*, 1973, 35: p. 550 (abstract).

difficulties. Nor indeed, it has to be said, was there initial, universal support from the medical profession who did not comprehend the need and were blinded by 'dog in the manger' attitudes.

In other areas, dedicated family practitioners belonging to the British Association for Immediate Care (BASIC) provided voluntary physician involvement in the pre-hospital care of trauma victims using their own equipment and working closely with their colleagues in the ambulance and other rescue services. BASICS only received modest funding from the DHSS for this work for a number of years and this has now been withdrawn. In 1986 a national programme of extended training to approximately paramedic standards for selected ambulance men was finally approved by the DHSS. This programme is gradually being implemented and we are now progressing towards a guaranteed nationwide service of a reasonable standard.

The Confidential Enquiry into Perioperative Deaths (CEPOD) published in 1987 brought matters to a head when it showed that a significant number of victims of trauma suffered avoidable deaths in hospital because of lack of resources and, importantly, because management of the seriously injured was often by relatively inexperienced medical staff without senior colleague involvement.

Moreover, Britain's trauma service was criticised by outside observers. Trunkey described the system in the UK as 'disorganised, fragmented and producing a universally bad outcome.' Trunkey is a surgeon respected worldwide for his demonstration of the value of a single hospital specialising in trauma care compared with smaller emergency departments allied to district hospitals. In a well planned study[1] he and his colleagues in San Francisco had shown that only one per cent of deaths from trauma were adjudged to be preventable in the trauma centre compared with between 28 per cent and 73 per cent in the ordinary hospitals. Many supportive studies had followed demonstrating the impact of trauma centres on preventable death and the concept had been

---

[1] West, J., Trunkey, D.D., Lim, R.C., 'System of Trauma Care', *Archives of Surgery*, 1979, 114: pp. 445-460.

further developed throughout the USA by the initiative of the American College of Surgeons' Committee on Trauma.

Retrospective and Prospective Studies

Stimulated by this evidence and the ostensibly justified criticism of the service in the UK, the Royal College of Surgeons of England (RCS) set up, through its Commission on the Provision of Surgical Services, a Working Party under the chairmanship of Professor Miles Irving to assess 'The Management of Patients with Major Injuries'. The report was published in November 1988.[1] The Working Party reviewed Britain's current service in the light of reported and first-hand experience in other countries, notably the USA, West Germany and France. They then commissioned a retrospective study of 1,000 deaths from injury in 11 Coroner's districts in England and Wales (100 cases from nine districts and 50 from two other districts). The districts were selected to include a spectrum of major cities, provincial towns and rural areas. Patients over 65 with fractured neck of femur were excluded from the study. The data from each fatality were studied by four assessors—three consultant surgeons and one accident and emergency consultant. All were familiar with the USA-style trauma centre. In their study of each case they were asked to address the question 'If this patient had been admitted to a fully staffed and equipped American-style trauma centre, might death have been prevented?' Analysis of the data revealed that 71 per cent of those who died were male and 49 per cent died at the scene or during transport to hospital.

There was, however, a wide variation in the proportion who died before admission to hospital (23-74 per cent) and, while a number of factors could be involved in this discrepancy, it is likely that differing standards of pre-hospital care was one of them. 514 patients were admitted to hospital and died subsequently—65 per

---

[1] Royal College of Surgeons of England Report of the Working Party, *The Management of Patients with Major Injuries*, Royal College of Surgeons of England, 1988.

cent as a result of central nervous system (CNS) (mainly brain) injury and the remainder (175 cases) from other injuries.

A substantial number of the deaths among those who arrived at hospital alive were adjudged to be preventable by the assessors. All four assessors agreed that 20 per cent had suffered preventable deaths, three out of four assessors put the figure at 34 per cent, and two out of four assessors at 47 per cent.

Most of the preventable deaths occurred in the non-CNS group. Overall, 43 per cent of this group were judged to be preventable by all assessors. One third of this cohort died within four hours and a further one third died during the first week in hospital. Half of the preventable deaths were due to misdiagnosis of relatively common conditions, such as ruptured liver, spleen and lacerated lung and subdural brain haemorrhage. Many died without operation or after an inadequate or inappropriate operation. The other common cause of preventable death was airway obstruction or inadequate respiration (15 per cent). There did not appear to be a significant difference in standard of treatment between teaching and non-teaching hospitals.

To supplement this retrospective study, the RCS Working Party undertook a prospective study of 150 patients admitted to four hospitals.[1] Two of the hospitals were teaching hospitals and two were non-teaching district general hospitals. 70 per cent of the patients were male and 60 per cent aged less than 40. One third of the injuries involved the CNS (mainly the brain). Only 11 per cent of these patients were seen initially by a doctor holding the rank of senior registrar or consultant. Of the 71 patients needing an operation only four had a consultant present during the procedure, presumably because of other commitments.

Thirty-two patients (21 per cent) died. All patients were analyzed according to the TRISS Index, which correlates the anatomical injury, the physiological deficit, and certain other factors such as age and produces a probability of living or dying according to proper practice. This probability can then be compared with the

---

[1] Spence, M.T., Redmond, A.D., Edwards, J.D., *Trauma Audit—The Use of TRISS Health Trends, 1988*, 3:(20), pp. 94-97.

actual outcome. Very few patients with a probability of survival of less than 50 per cent recovered but one third of those who died had a recovery probability of more than 50 per cent. This investigation complements the retrospective study in highlighting the suboptimal standards of treatment of trauma victims and emphasises the lack of experienced senior medical involvement in the early phase of management.

A further prospective study undertaken by the University Hospital of South Manchester and Stockport Health Authority analyzed the results from patients treated in a district general hospital and a teaching hospital with excellent facilities using the TRISS system to calculate survival probability. Both hospitals lost patients they should not have done (the teaching hospital proportionately more than the district general hospital). However, as if to make up for this, the teaching hospital did save a number of patients with a very low probability of survival (e.g. six per cent and 15 per cent). These unexpected survivors received prompt treatment by a consultant and full resuscitative, investigative, surgical and intensive care facilities were immediately available. They demonstrate the benefits of a properly managed and equipped trauma service.

Further evidence comes from workers in Belfast[1] who compared the outcome of two cohorts of patients. In one group the junior accident and emergency doctors used the Revised Trauma Score system to identify those with serious injuries (TRISS greater than 15) and on the basis of the score, followed protocols to call in experienced senior assistance immediately to supervise resuscitation. This simple additional triage tool enabled management errors to be reduced from 59 per cent to 30 per cent but, of course, relied on senior help being readily and rapidly available supported by the necessary facilities and equipment.

These well conducted scientific studies make disturbing reading and reinforce the view that Trunkey was, at least in part, right in

---

[1] Fisher, R.B. & Dearden, C.H., 'Improving the Care of Major Trauma Victims in the Accident and Emergency Department', *British Medical Journal*, 16 June 1990, vol. 300, pp. 1560-63.

his criticism of the UK trauma service. Clearly, many of the problems that he had demonstrated in the US in the seventies, which had been dramatically improved by a reorganised and revitalised service there, also applied to the United Kingdom.

The Solutions

Prevention must be the ultimate method of reducing the incidence of trauma and there is no doubt that the compulsory wearing of seat belts, motor cycle crash helmets, and the Health & Safety at Work Regulations have eliminated many deaths and serious injuries.

Further modest improvements will arise as a result of safer car design, improved roads, stricter alcohol consumption control, better education of drivers and pedestrians, and safer home appliances. However, these measures take a long time to generate and implement and are likely to have only marginal impact on the overall figures. Relying upon Parliament to introduce new legislation rapidly in this field is unrealistic judging by the past record of a delay of many years in introducing front and rear seat belt requirements.

We must assume, therefore, that there will always be a substantial number of victims of trauma and should take steps now to improve their standard of treatment, which is clearly below par.

The key recommendations of the Royal College of Surgeons Working Party are summarised below.

1. The majority of injured patients should be managed in large district general hospitals with a wide range of facilities and experienced staff and an Accident and Emergency Department supervised by Consultants in accident and emergency medicine.

2. The accident and emergency services should be situated in only one hospital per NHS district, so concentrating resources and experience.

3. Patients with life-threatening injuries outside the capability of the district general hospital should be transferred or brought directly to a trauma centre situated alongside an

Accident and Emergency Department based at a large hospital which can provide a 24-hour service by senior specialists in accident and emergency medicine, anaesthesia, general, orthopaedic, neuro, cardiothoracic, vascular, maxillo-facial and plastic surgery, radiology and haematology and their supporting services. Facilities should be available for immediate sophisticated resuscitation and surgery. It is estimated that one trauma centre would service several NHS districts and a population of 1.5 to 2 million.

4. Pre-hospital care should be provided by ambulance men trained to paramedic standards and, where available, by family practitioners trained in immediate care. All should be familiar with a scoring system and protocols to assist in selecting patients with serious injuries requiring the services of a trauma centre. There should be greater medical involvement in the organisation and training of the ambulance service.

5. Better transportation should be available and this should include the use of helicopters in appropriate circumstances to bring patients with major injuries directly from remote areas or transferring them from district general hospitals to trauma centres.

6. There is a need for a greater interest and better training in trauma in the appropriate specialties and at undergraduate level.

7. There is a need for audit of the care of trauma victims both in the pre-hospital phase and in hospital through national and international schemes so that standards in each individual centre can be regularly reviewed with the object of improving outcome.

8. Research investment into the causes, prevention and management of injury should be increased substantially.

Clearly these recommendations cannot be implemented without a radical change in attitudes, from the professions, from health care managers, from the Exchequer, from the politicians and from the public.

The Profession

Consultants in district general hospitals must be far sighted enough to abandon jealously guarded restrictive practices and co-operative with the concept of those few patients with major life-threatening and multiple injuries being treated at a trauma centre. It has been estimated that the proportion of these patients amounts to less than five per cent of the total number of injured patients seen at an accident and emergency department in a district general hospital so the overall workload at any centre would not be significantly affected.

A trauma centre cannot survive without sufficient patients to ensure continuing experience and economic use of the facilities and staff required. The minimum number of cases for viability is 300-400 per year and, currently, this number of major injuries occurs in association with a population of approximately 1.5 to 2 million. Senior medical staff will have to change their current practice of leaving the care of emergency patients to junior staff outside office hours. There are already signs that they are prepared to do this but not, reasonably enough, as an addition to their present workload. This will mean more appointments in accident and emergency medicine, anaesthesia, radiology and the appropriate surgical specialties in the hospitals designated as trauma centres. Hand in hand with this will be a requirement for an increase in trainees to fill these posts. Nevertheless, the increase will not have to be very dramatic since there will only need to be about 30 trauma centres in the UK. Two or three extra senior members of each specialty will be required to staff each centre.

One improvement in attitude could be made right away in large district general hospitals—an increased sense of urgency by junior hospital doctors in calling for help and an increased speed of response to that call by senior medical staff. When specialist help is called for it should be responded to at senior level—experienced registrar, senior registrar or consultant—not by a senior house officer with only a few months' experience. It is this ridiculous practice which causes fatal delay and creates avoidable deaths and disability.

The Managers

Managers at National, Regional and District levels must appreciate the current carnage caused by trauma and recognise the potential value of improved treatment. As such they must be prepared to realise the value of centralising the general trauma care within a district and creating a sub-regional centre for specialised care. Priorities should not be influenced by petty considerations of financial cross boundary flows currently prevalent.

As a start, a fully staffed operating room should be available 24 hours a day, set aside purely for the treatment of emergencies. Urgently needed surgery should not be delayed by lack of operating room space because all the facilities are in use for routine lists.[1] The object of having managers in the National Health Service is to create and expedite opportunities for better patient care—not to delay or obstruct such opportunities. Clear-cut cases of need and potential benefit need rapid and incisive decisions—the hallmark of good management in the commercial world. Paper and committees, and delays, cost a great deal in terms of both money and time and—in this instance lives—the case does not have to be re-made again and again at quarterly or six monthly intervals.

The Exchequer

The cost of better trauma care will, on first calculations, appear high. To add trauma centres to existing suitable hospitals will probably cost about £2 million to £3 million each. The national total will, therefore, amount to some £80 million. To staff and maintain these trauma centres will probably cost a further £1 million each, per year; say, £30 million nationally.

---

[1] *Report of the Working Party on Efficiency of Theatre Services*, Association of Anaesthetists of Great Britain and Ireland and The Association of Surgeons of Great Britain and Ireland 1989.

However, balanced against these expenditures must be set the cost of trauma victims to the nation. Taking the Department of Transport's figure of £500,000 per fatality, the bill for the nation annually for our 5,000 fatalities amounts to £2,500 million—for deaths arising from road accidents alone.

If we assume the most conservative figures from the Royal College Working Party retrospective study, where four out of four assessors agreed that 20 per cent of the deaths were avoidable, then around 1,000 lives could be saved each year. At £500,000 each, this amounts to £500 million—every year. Balanced against an initial outlay of £80 million and £30 million costs annually this has got to be one of the best investments ever in cash terms alone—leaving aside the 1,000 patients and their families who will be grateful.

Arguments that many who are saved will only live to be disabled can be countered by the knowledge that the majority of deaths classed as avoidable in the study were due to simple causes, such as haemorrhage and airway obstruction. If these conditions are treated appropriately, quality survival may be confidently expected. Additionally, a higher standard of trauma care will undoubtedly reduce the incidence of those who currently have preventable severe disability. Sadly, with our Government system, the costs come out of one waistcoat pocket and the savings go into another. It requires a far sighted Treasury to realise the potential benefit and the overall improvement which would be seen when the books were balanced at the end of the year.

There are other sources of funds which could be tapped. A one per cent levy on car and life insurance premiums could produce £50 million to £100 million annually and would be good value for the insurers. A five per cent levy on the Road Vehicle Licence Tax would produce a very substantial sum, easily covering the costs of better trauma care. Few car owners would complain if their Road Vehicle Licence went up from £100 to £105 for this reason.

It would, of course, be vital that these sums were directly apportioned to the cause for which they were given and not mixed in with general exchequer, or overall NHS funds. There is also a need for a trauma orientated charity organisation analogous to the

British Heart Foundation or the many cancer fund-raising bodies who have, respectively, £21 million and £100 million to spend on research in 1990.[1] Amazingly, no similar body existed to support trauma care research until The Trauma Foundation was launched in early 1991. This is perhaps because trauma is a disease affecting those at a stage of their life when they have little cash to spare for charity. And yet, they are the nation's life blood and future. This foundation should be supported by all.

The Politicians

The Royal College Working Party Report was received with interest by the then Minister of Health, Mr David Mellor, in November 1988. Correctly he sought opinion from all relevant bodies in the medical profession and allied groups.

All respondents agreed that the standard of trauma care in the United Kingdom, at best, left a lot to be desired. Not all agreed that trauma centres should be established nationwide immediately, but all agreed that some centres (say five) should be set up to see if the benefits experienced in the USA, Germany and France would also apply to Britain. One suspects that some of the responses were influenced by the supposition that full funding of a nationwide service would be ruled out of the question and it would be more realistic to hope for the traditional British half a loaf. The medical profession has become accustomed to the 'we can't afford it' response and in a Pavlovian, think small, manner seek the compromise first, rather than the full price and the full benefit.

As a result, the Department of Health has supported the establishment of but one trauma centre, at Stoke, which will be assessed over a period of years. Surely it would have been better to fund a few more to analyse a more widespread experience across the nation.

Meanwhile more than 100 people die every month, unnecessarily, at vast expense. Shall we have to wait a decade for yet another

---

[1] Cummins, B.H., Personal communication.

report to highlight our continuing shortcomings? Or, is it too much to hope that the electorate, the long-suffering, excessively tolerant and apathetic 'British public' might give a prod in the right direction to our politicians, now?

3

The Organisation of Accident Services

B. McKibbin

There appears to be general recognition of the important role which injuries play in causing death and disablement in the community. The gloomy litany of road traffic statistics is often repeated and the additional role of injury at work and even in the home is well recognised. Since injury is widely perceived to be the most obvious of preventable diseases it is not surprising that these figures have prompted considerable research and effort into the prevention of accidents. However, the magnitude of these figures indicates that this has been far from completely successful and it is surprising therefore that there is not an equal interest in the management of injuries when they do occur.

Problems of Public Awareness

It would be too much to suggest that the public is satisfied with the present accident services but they do appear to complain about them less often compared with some other aspects of the health service and in the recent proposals to restructure the latter they received scarcely a mention. One reason for this is that the service on the whole is promptly available, at least for major injuries, and there are of course no waiting lists which are the main bone of contention. However, patients are not always able to assess whether the quality of the care given is the best available and many deficiencies may go unrecognised. These are more readily apparent to those who are responsible for the delivery of the service and it is probably for this reason that most of the criticisms of it have come from within their ranks. Ever since the last war, a series of reports has been produced on accident services by a variety of professional bodies. These have varied in the detail of their conclusions but they have been unanimous in concluding that a more structured and centralised service is desirable and the setting up of specialised accident units of one form or another have been generally recommended. In spite of the fact that some of these reports were commissioned and accepted by the Government of the day little or no action has been taken to implement them.

The probable reason for this is that there has been no pressure to do so from the public at large who have not been convinced that such developments are in their interest; indeed such proposals are often violently opposed. At the time of writing there are several examples of small towns calling for their own neighbourhood accident service usually aided and abetted by their member of Parliament but opposed by medical opinion. This is understandable since centralised units inevitably mean more travelling which is inconvenient for patients with minor injuries and many find it difficult to accept that a longer ambulance journey is not prejudicial to a critically injured patient.

The Solution: Concentration of Services

However the evidence does not support this view. Although many of the earlier reports relied largely on the opinion of admittedly experienced senior clinicians, in recent times more scientific studies have become available and the concept of the 'preventable death' in trauma has been developed. Studies carried out, initially in the United States, have shown that where there is an organised trauma centre with a team of senior doctors available 24 hours a day the incidence of such deaths is significantly reduced compared with the results achieved by more scattered individual units. Furthermore, when these latter were amalgamated or closed the death rate fell.

Report by the Royal College of Surgeons of England

Similar results have been reported from Canada and West Germany and more recently these studies have been extended to the United Kingdom. In 1988 the Royal College of Surgeons produced their report on the management of major injuries[1] which included a retrospective review of the trauma deaths in a wide selection of hospitals. This revealed that as many as one third of these could possibly have been prevented and that the main cause of these deficiencies was that there were too many inefficient, inadequately staffed accident units lacking adequate consultant supervision. Their main recommendations were that the resources to cope with major injuries should be concentrated and there should only be one hospital with an accident and emergency department in each National Health Service district. Other services in the same district should be closed or their freedom to treat the injured restricted. In addition, they felt that there should be provision of regional trauma centres to deal with the most severe injuries with the objective of providing essentially a consultant-based service 24 hours a day to a population of about two million. They recommended that these latter units should be staffed by a multidisciplinary *team* and specifically rejected the concept of an all-purpose accident surgeon. They also emphasised the need for more research money to be diverted to the pre-hospital care of the injured.

There is therefore general professional agreement that trauma services should be more concentrated and any continuing debate concerns only the scale on which that should occur. Different groups of surgeons tend to see the problem in the light of their own particular specialty. Understandably, those who deal with relatively few cases such as cardiovascular surgeons would like to see concentration on a larger scale so that enough cases are available to run an efficient service. Orthopaedic surgeons, on the

---

[1] Royal College of Surgeons of England Report of the Working Party, *The Management of Patients with Major Injuries*, Royal College of Surgeons of England, 1988.

other hand who deal with the majority of accidents see the issue as being rather more complicated.

The Orthopaedic Surgeons Role

Serious injuries to the head, chest and abdomen may present the most urgent of surgical emergencies but numerically they are very small compared with skeletal injuries. In the recent M1 air disaster the Queen's Medical Centre, Nottingham, carried out 55 emergency operations, of which only two were abdominal, two were for head injury and one for facial injury, while the remaining 50 were orthopaedic. When less serious injuries are considered the disproportion is even greater: in our own large accident centre in Cardiff, which serves a population of over 350,000, about 8,000 fractures are treated in a year, of which over 2,000 are operated on. During the same period, less than 50 abdominal procedures are required for trauma. Although skeletal injuries can be life threatening the majority are not; but they are on the other hand capable of producing significant disability with resulting suffering and loss of time from employment. Because they are so numerous the effect of inadequate treatment would be to put an enormous burden on the Community.

The methods of fracture management have changed very greatly over the past fifty years. Formerly only difficult injuries were operated upon, the majority being treated by so-called 'conservative' or closed methods with plaster casts, splints and the use of in-patient traction. The typical cartoonists representation of an accident ward depicts patients with their legs swathed in large bandages suspended from pieces of string and this is a relic of that era. A visit to a modern accident ward will reveal an entirely different scene, traction cords are rarely in view and most of the patients will either be mobile or in the process of becoming so. This has come about as the result of improvements in the operative treatment of fractures with plates, screws and other devices. Twenty years ago a young man with a fractured thigh bone could expect to remain in hospital for three months on traction and to attend the physiotherapy department for another two months. He would be unlikely to return to any form of work before six months and his absence might be much more prolonged than that. Using modern techniques he might expect to remain in hospital only ten days and to be able to return to some forms of work within two months.

However, the earlier closed methods of treatment were comparatively safe and could often be safely delegated to juniors in the knowledge that any mistakes could be subsequently retrieved by another more experienced hand. It was common therefore for one surgeon to be responsible for a very large number of patients exercising a largely supervisory role. Before the last war in some of our large cities all the fractures were overseen by a mere handful of surgeons often in a whole variety of different hospitals. Such treatment did not require complicated equipment and it could be carried out in comparatively small hospitals which were often conveniently near to the patient's home.

It is obvious that such an arrangement is incompatible with modern operative fracture treatment and yet the previous order of things still has a considerable influence in the arrangements which obtain today. The management of fractures is often seen as a mere sideline to an orthopaedic surgeon's duties which are mainly concerned with reconstructive surgery so that orthopaedic surgeons are often still required to supervise fracture treatment in more than one hospital. In many of the smaller accident units there are only two surgeons who have between them to provide a 24-hour service, including cover for their own illness and holidays, as well as carrying out a full complement of reconstructive work. The operative treatment of fractures is now very complicated requiring the highest degree of surgical skill so that, unlike the older methods, it cannot safely be delegated to juniors. Nevertheless the number of consultant orthopaedic surgeons in Britain is only one third of the numbers obtaining in most European countries when related to population, and the comparison with the U.S.A. and Australia is even more unfavourable.

Under these conditions it is obviously very difficult to realise the full potential of modern treatment methods. Because of these misgivings the British Orthopaedic Association set up a review by a panel of surgeons to comment on the standard of care given to a number of injured patients selected at random from all over the country. This showed, rather depressingly, that in 22 per cent of cases the treatment was judged to be seriously deficient. In about half of these the cause was thought to be the lack of involvement of a sufficiently senior doctor, while in the remainder it was felt that transfer to a more specialised centre would have been advisable.

Report By The British Orthopaedic Association

As a result of this and other studies, the Association has produced its own report on the management of trauma.[1] The Association supported the College of Surgeons views that larger units were needed although they had some reservations as to the need for the very large regional units envisaged in the College report. They emphasised their concern for the lesser injuries by concentrating more on the changes at the lower levels of the service and these detailed recommendations will now be considered.

District General Hospitals

The district general hospital is the workhorse of the NHS and there may be several of these in any one Health Service District depending on its size. More than one may have an accident unit. This is particularly so in the larger cities where a patient with a fracture may have the choice of several hospitals offering a 24-hour service. Although an element of choice may be considered desirable this possible advantage is neutralized if the treatment offered at all the hospitals is inadequate. Such an arrangement is clearly inefficient both with regard to manpower and equipment and the British Orthopaedic Association has endorsed the recommendation of the College of Surgeons that there should only be one hospital in a district which should be designated as a trauma centre. It is not suggested that the units should close at the other hospitals but rather that they should be restricted in the services they offer so that the more serious injuries would be passed on to the designated hospital.

---

[1] Trauma Sub-committee of the British Orthopaedic Association, *The Management of Trauma in Great Britain*, British Orthodpaedic Association, London: 1989.

This policy has important implications for the ambulance services which would be placed in the position of having to make a decision about the severity of the injury and then perhaps bringing the patient directly to the designated hospital. This could involve taking a severely injured patient past the doors of a hospital which in the past had offered a full accident service. This is the aspect of the arrangement for which it is most difficult to gain acceptance both from the public and the ambulance service and even from some medical practitioners. However, experience in other parts of the world has shown that it does work, although the ambulance service itself must be upgraded. At the very least it is necessary to involve paramedics who can be trained to assess the severity of injury and also to initiate resuscitation. Any delays produced by this will be more than offset by the improved treatment available at the designated hospital.

Minor Injury Units
These are units that exist outside a district general hospital, usually in community hospitals, and are often manned on a part-time basis by general practitioners. Again, their role is controversial; it is often pointed out with justice that there is no such thing as a minor injury by which it is meant that any minor injury can become a major problem if it is not properly managed. For that reason some feel that minor injury units should be closed and all patients directed to a larger unit. Such a policy is likely to be highly unpopular with the public who will rightly feel that they should receive attention for these injuries without travelling inconvenient distances, once again demonstrating the difficulty of reconciling convenience of care with the maintenance of adequate standards. However, with proper supervision, the latter can be enforced. These departments should not be independent units but should be under the aegis of the accident and emergency department of a district general hospital. They should be visited regularly by a consultant from that unit and ideally junior staff should rotate between the units. A very tight operational policy needs to be drawn up indicating the type of injuries which may be treated and a backup radiological reporting service is essential. Under these conditions these units have been shown to work well.

Regional Trauma Centres

The advantage of such regional centres is that they can bring under one roof all the disciplines necessary to treat seriously injured patients including orthopaedic and general surgeons, cardiac and neurosurgeons together with plastic surgeons. Senior surgeons can be available, on a rota basis, round the clock. The concept of a multidisciplinary team has now prevailed against an earlier idea that surgeons should specialise in the treatment of trauma in all parts of the body so that the same surgeon might open the abdomen for a ruptured spleen, internally fix a fracture and decompress an intracranial bleed. This latter arrangement is obviously more efficient in terms of manpower, especially when a rostered 24-hour service is needed, but because of the increasing complexity of the techniques used in the various disciplines it is now considered that it would be very difficult for any one man to master all of these as in former times. The disadvantage of the team approach is that it is inefficient. Multiple injuries unfortunately do not present at regular intervals so that there would inevitably be times when this large and expensive team would be inactive. It could of course be argued that this is a disadvantage which is accepted for the Fire Brigade and other Rescue Services so why not for the accident services also?

However, from the point of view of the majority of skeletal injuries the participation of a full range of other specialties on site is not essential and most of these could be adequately treated in a designated district general hospital as described above. The number of cases would be sufficiently large to employ senior surgeons almost exclusively for their management. Such surgeons could then specialise in this field thus raising the standard of treatment for the most difficult injuries, which at the present time have to take their chances at the local district general hospital. The question then arises as to whether such hospitals can offer an adequate level of care for the much less common but life threatening multiple injuries. Comprehensive hard data relating to this issue are not yet available but there are in existence a number of larger fracture units serving populations of up to half a million and preventable death audits are beginning to appear from some of these. The results appear to be very much more acceptable than those studied in the College of Surgeons report suggesting that the additional benefit to be gained from an effective quadrupling of the drainage area of these units into a Regional Centre is likely to be marginal and may not justify the additional cost. However, the Department of Health has already sponsored a pilot project with the creation of a single large unit in Stoke-on-Trent and further developments must await the results from that experiment. Orthopaedic surgeons are by no means opposed to these developments, at least in the larger conurbations, but they are concerned that a continuing debate about their cost effectiveness might distract attention from the benefits which would follow for the great majority of patients from the less radical changes which they have proposed at a more local level.

Financial Considerations

All new developments cost money and the cost benefit considerations surrounding large regional trauma centres have already been touched upon. Nevertheless the costs may well be less than they appear at first sight. These trauma patients are being treated at the present time and costs are already incurred. By locating them onto fewer sites there may well be savings in equipment and manpower costs, which will depend on the extent of the 'Fire Brigade' effect. However, this problem needs to be considered in a wider context. A famous Swiss orthopaedic surgeon described the purpose of good trauma management as 'returning the patient to tax paying status'. A patient who dies due to mismanagement shortly after hospital admission may actually save the hospital money by freeing it from the necessity to continue his treatment and prolonged convalescence. But, leaving aside humanitarian considerations, any saving would soon be overtaken by the cost to the state of maintaining his family during what would have been the rest of his working life. The cost may come out of a different pocket at the Treasury but it is in the end the State which bears all. Similar considerations apply to almost all injuries; prior to the last war it was entirely understood by everyone that if a working man broke his thigh his working days were at an end. Nowadays the cost of nailing his femur would be paid for many times over by the tax that he will contribute during the rest of his working life. The writer lacks the necessary actuarial skills even to begin to compute this on a nationwide basis but the sums involved must be enormous. Unfortunately, such arguments appeal little to local Treasurers who have short term budgets to balance in a limited field and are no more appealing to politicians whose temporal perspective is unlikely to extend beyond the next general election.

The Way Forward

Progress to date in the improvement of trauma services has been disappointing for those involved. Study after study has been produced but in spite of there being a consistent message little action has followed. Even the government's response to the recent College of Surgeons report has been miserly, with limited funding being given to one experimental unit. The allocation of research funds follows the same pattern. Although trauma is one of the commonest causes of death, only a fraction of the funds devoted to topics such as heart disease and cancer is given to trauma research, in spite of the enormous potential for improvement. It is not likely that anything will change unless there is a radical improvement in the general public's awareness of the problem. Only when they perceive the need for reorganisation and improvement will there be pressure on governments to act. A major public relations exercise is required to convince them that convenience and local availability of treatment may have to be sacrificed in the interests of a better standard of care. Only then will the energies currently expended on campaigns for the opening of yet more small accident units be channelled into a drive for properly organised major accident units.